Introduction

In the course of compiling this book I spoke to a number of directors working in various areas of theatre, from drama schools to the National Theatre. Nearly everyone agreed that an actor's most important attribute was self-knowledge. Self-knowledge can be expressed in a variety of ways: through wit, intelligence, verbal and physical dexterity, an assertive, as opposed to an aggressive manner.

There is a great difference in approach to auditioning in Britain and the United States. In America cut-throat competition has engendered a highly professional attitude. Actors tend to arrive fully prepared for an audition, on time, with well-rehearsed speeches from plays that they have taken the time to read in their entirety. In contrast directors spoke about the appalling diffidence of many actors in Britain, who arrived in no way prepared, appearing to feel that the audition was something of an imposition and that performing was the last thing in the world they wanted to do.

Directors were keen to emphasize the fact that an audition is not a test but a meeting between the actor and director to assess the possibility of working together. Many felt that auditioning should be more of a two-way process and that actors should accept more power or responsibility for themselves when auditioning. In other words, actors should not be tempted to play down their own intelligence, to act according to what they think the director wants, but to see themselves as professionals.

Opinions differ as to how much an actor can show about the way he/she works in an audition. One felt that it was a genuine opportunity for an actor to display their work; another, that little could actually be revealed by the presentation of a speech – auditioning being an artificial performing situation – and that the actor should concentrate on presenting *themselves* as well as possible, on maximizing their presence. Clearly in an ideal audition one should do both. One should be clear, concise and, equally important, unpretentious. One director talked of avoiding the temptation to be arch. Another was looking for 'assurance with natural reticence', which she went on to explain as including the director in the audition in an open way, talking with, rather than at, him or her.

Most key points as regards the selection and presentation of the audition piece are common sense, but easy to overlook in the attempt to impress. For instance it would be unwise to attempt a speech using a particular accent unless it was well within your capabilities and it would be sensible to choose a role within your own age-range. In the event of an audition being for a specific role, select a pertinent piece: if the production is to be a comedy, present a comic speech. It should be emphasized that there is no substitute, when preparing an audition speech, for reading the play in its entirety.

Everybody acknowledged the advantages of doing a witty or comic piece mainly because they enjoyed being able to laugh. They felt that it was extremely hard for an actor to play a highly emotional scene in an audition without resorting to a good deal of tension, both physically and vocally.

How can you make auditioning a less nerve-racking affair? Most directors agreed on this. Get a good night's sleep, wear comfortable clothes, arrive early and find a quiet place to calm down and 'centre' yourself. Above all, everyone stressed, *have fun*!

Three women factory workers are made redundant just before Christmas. Marje's husband is already unemployed and the strain and humiliation he is suffering has led him into beating Marje. She is persuaded by the youngest of the three to come down to London for a few weeks to work as a prostitute in order to be able to provide her family with a proper Christmas.

This speech takes place on the journey down to King's Cross, London from Manchester. Marje is, in effect, talking to herself.

Thatcher's Women *by Kay Adshead*

Marje Sunday afternoons . . . George Formby on the telly. The long bus ride to me grandma's house. She'd lived in that house since she was married, before that she'd lived in the same house two streets away . . . all the houses in all the streets, two-ups, two-downs, streets and streets, built for the mill, for me grandma was a mill hand.

At six o'clock, the mill siren would stop the dreams in the mill houses and send hundreds on the long misty trudge up Pigalle Hill.

When the mill closed down my grandma went to work at the shirt factory on the buttonholing machine. In the war she worked in the munitions factory making bombs, then went back to the buttonholing, then they put her on collar and cuffs – then on shirt tails – round hemming.

Two-ups, two-downs – white stone steps. Parlour with the pot shepherd boy, hands in his pockets, whistling – the back room where my grandma sat, the scullery, backyard, outside lav, yard door, opening on to the entry. . . . On the other side of the entry was a brick wall, 20–30–40 feet, on the top, sharpened steel rods, and barbed wire – for the houses backed on to Belle Vue. (*The train picks up speed.*)

At the front, on the road, there was a green arch with blue and yellow letters: 'Welcome to Belle Vue Zoo'. There was a kiddie's playground with plaster giraffes and monkeys and hippos, and concrete tubs full of geraniums, and on bank holidays a man dressed up as a clown handing out balloons.

From the house there was just the great brick wall.

On the other side of the wall was the lion house, the tiger house, the elephant house.

Sitting in the back room with my grandma, watching George Formby on the telly, we would hear the low roars and bellows, the pounding and threshing of wild creatures.

One Sunday afternoon, we heard a great scream over our heads, over all the streets and houses. One of the lions – or tigers – or leopards – had looked at the brick wall and the sharpened steel rods and the barbed wire – and remembered.

3

A group of university graduates return to their old halls for a college reunion. They are now all highly respected members of the Establishment. As the evening commences they gradually revert to their student personas – revealing how misconceived were their notions of themselves and each other. Lady Driver, now the Master's wife, was married to Roddy who is absent from the reunion. However, Lady Driver is unaware of this fact as she confronts the man whom she believes to be Roddy in his darkened room.

Donkey's Years *by Michael Frayn*

Lady Driver   Brown corduroy trousers. I'd forgotten your brown
corduroy trousers. They can't be the same brown corduroy trousers you
were wearing that weekend we stayed at the Ritz . . . (*Starting to cry.*)

I'm sorry, Roddy. I can't help it. It's the trousers. It's just suddenly
coming face to face with your brown corduroy trousers in there when
I'd forgotten about them. Thrown down all over the floor with no legs
inside them. . . . Just don't say anything. And don't look at me. If you
just leave me alone for a minute I'll be alright . . . I didn't plan this, of
course, I didn't plan to walk in after 17 years and burst into tears. It
was just seeing the trousers half on the bed and half off, and one sock on
the washstand . . . It was just having to wait in the bedroom while
everyone was shouting in here . . . I didn't plan to be in the bedroom, of
course. It didn't occur to me that you might bring back some horde of
people here after dinner. Didn't you think I might be here? Didn't it
cross your mind that I might be waiting somewhere? Or have you just
completely forgotten about me . . . ? Look I'm not crying because of
you. I didn't come to have some terrible nostalgic scene, because I
don't feel like that about it. I never think about the past. I'm far too
busy with the present. I lead a very active life. I just came to see how
you were and to tell you how I was, and I'm fine, I'm very happy,
things have turned out very well for me, and all I'm crying about is that
I have to stand and tell you all this while I'm crying . . . The sound of
you jumping to wrong conclusions is deafening. . . . Now you won't
even look at me. You won't say anything. One of your famous silences.
That's why everyone was always so impressed by you – because you
just stood there and grinned and said nothing . . . I'm not angry about
what happened. I can see it was my fault. But I wasn't really going to
walk out! I came back to the hotel that night and you'd gone. I know I
said I was going to walk out. But you hadn't said a word all the way
from Tripoli to Tunis! Somebody had to say something! I know I took
all the money – but that was so you couldn't leave. It's just that I met
these people I knew, and I went to have a drink with them, and so on,
and so forth, and when I got back you'd gone, and all the rest of it, and
obviously the postcard I sent to explain about everything only got to
you after the engagement had been announced in *The Times*. . . .
Anyway I've changed. I've become very punctilious among other
things. Perhaps because of the mistake I made with you. You may not
believe this, but I often think about what happened. I often think about
you. . . . Oh God, I shouldn't have come. I see now, it's disastrous. The
whole plan's gone wrong.

Joyriders is set in Belfast, where a group of young offenders are taking part in a government Youth Opportunities Programme. The aim of the scheme is to provide them with 'helpful' skills enabling them to find employment at the end of the year.

Maureen is sweet, naïve – and innocent. She lives alone with her younger brother Johnny, a habitual glue-sniffer and joy-rider. Maureen is pregnant by a university student, a fact she has kept secret from everyone but her friend Sandra.

Sandra has just left the room, taunting Maureen with the prospect of swollen ankles now that she is pregnant. Maureen responds by half-answering Sandra and half-talking to her unborn child.

Joyriders *by Christina Reid*

Maureen There's nuthin' the matter with my ankles . . .

She begins to work the knitting machine, stops, looks down.

Don't heed her baby . . . he loves me . . . I know he does . . . he said he
did . . . and he's a gentleman . . .

She operates the knitting machine again, stops.

We're gonna live in an old house behind the university . . . and every
day I'll put you in your pram and wheel you round the Botanic
Gardens . . . a proper pram . . . Silver Cross with big high wheels . . .
and everybody'll look at you, you'll be that beautiful . . . your father's
dark eyes an' your granny's blonde hair . . .

She stops at the thought of her mother. **Sandra** *comes in, sets the milk down,
watches and listens to* **Maureen** *who doesn't see her.*

Your granny was like the sun . . . all golden . . . she lit up everything
she touched . . . she come from the country and got cooped up in the
flats like a battery hen . . . the day your granda went to England to look
for work, we were that miserable she took me an' Johnnie to the
pictures . . . The Wizard of Oz . . . it was lovely . . . an' the next day she
bought seven pot plants . . . seven . . . an' she put them in a row on the
kitchen window sill an' she said . . . 'They'll all flower except for the
fourth one. That one has to stay green.' And she wouldn't tell us why.
'Wait and see' she said . . . 'Wait and see.' We watched an' we waited
for a while an' nuthin' happened, an' we lost interest. Didn't even
notice them any more. And then one day I come in from school an' all
the pot plants had flowers except the fourth one, just like she said.

She smiles and counts on her fingers.

Red, orange, yellow, green, blue, indigo, violet . . . 'See' she said, 'we
have a rainbow on our window sill.'

She looks round, sees **Sandra**.

You come in that day . . . do you remember?

Fear and Misery . . . is a series of short scenes showing how all strata of society in Germany were affected by the mistrust and violence bred by the Nazi regime.

A Jewish wife, married to a gentile doctor in Germany in the nineteen thirties, is preparing to flee from the growing Nazi persecution. Before her husband arrives home from work she rehearses to herself how she will break the news of her departure to him.

Fear And Misery In The Third Reich
by Bertolt Brecht

Jewish Wife   Yes, I'm packing. Don't pretend you haven't noticed
anything the last few days. Nothing really matters, Fritz, except just
one thing: if we spend our last hour together without looking at each
other's eyes. That's a triumph they can't be allowed, the liars who
force everyone else to lie. Ten years ago when somebody said no one
would think I was Jewish, you instantly said yes, they would. And
that's fine. That was straightforward. Why take things in a roundabout
way now? I'm packing so they shan't take away your job as senior
physician. And because they've stopped saying good morning to you at
the clinic, and because you're not sleeping nowadays. I don't want you
to tell me I mustn't go. And I'm hurrying because I don't want to hear
you telling me I must. It's a matter of time. Principles are a matter of
time. They don't last for ever, any more than a glove does. (There are
good ones which last a long while. But even they only have a certain
life.) Don't get the idea that I'm angry. Yes, I am. Why should I always
be understanding? What's wrong with the shape of my nose and the
colour of my hair? I'm to leave the town where I was born just so they
don't have to go short of butter. What sort of people are you, yourself
included? You work out the quantum theory and the Trendelenburg
test, then allow a lot of semi-barbarians to tell you you're to conquer
the world but you can't have the woman you want. The artificial lung,
and the dive-bomber! You are monsters or you pander to monsters.
Yes, I know I'm being unreasonable, but what good is reason in a
world like this? There you sit watching your wife pack and saying
nothing.

In a gynaecological ward, Chris, a thirty-year-old woman hoping to have an operation to 'cure' her infertility, meets Eileen, a young girl having an abortion, and they become friends.

Chris is a warm, humorous and unsentimental woman who longs to have a child. She is very protective and understanding towards Eileen and in no way condemns her for wanting to have an abortion. In this speech she reveals why.

Raspberry *by Tony Marchant*

Chris Have I?

Pause.

When I was eighteen, a year older than you – I went to a private clinic.
Stayed overnight. (. . .) None of my family knew I was there. I was
terrified – I held this lucky charm in my hand – so tightly the knuckles
turned white. The room was very nice – it had a television and a
telephone and the nurse brought me a cup of tea on a tray. Fifty pounds
they charged. I got a sub on me wages. You went private then – even
though a law had been passed a couple of years before for it to be done
on the National Health, hospitals were refusing or making it very hard.
Aggravation. Then there was the big risk that your family might find
out. Girls who it was known had had abortions got pointed at in the
street, became notorious. It was a terrible thing. At the clinic they were
mostly interested in your fifty pounds.

Pause.

1970 that was – I bought a trouser suit that year, trying to look older
than I was. Pale pink lipstick, black eyes. Still loved Tamla Motown –
Diana Ross hadn't long left the Supremes. *Ain't No Mountain High
Enough* she was singing. Jackson Five had just come out. The boy's
name was Mark – I thought he was tasty because he was growing his
sideburns long. He didn't want to know. (. . .)
  Felt lonely waiting for the bus home next day. And it was so cold and
I couldn't walk properly because it hurt too much. I bought a walnut
whip to cheer myself up. I was sick in the kerb. Me mum thought I
looked a bit peeky. Something I ate round Sharon's last night I said.
Sharon was my alibi.

Educating Rita is a two-hander following the relationship between Rita, a bright Liverpudlian hairdresser, and her Open University English professor, Frank. As the course progresses Rita's passion to find herself a 'better life' has a profound effect upon the world-weary tutor.

In this speech Rita attempts to explain to Frank why she felt unable to come to a party at his home.

Educating Rita *by Willy Russell*

Rita *(angrily)* But I don't wanna be charming and delightful: funny. What's funny? I don't wanna be funny. I wanna talk seriously with the rest of you, I don't wanna spend the night takin' the piss, comin' on with the funnies because that's the only way I can get into the conversation. I didn't want to come to your house just to play the court jester. (. . .)

But I don't want to be myself. Me? What's me? Some stupid woman who gives us all a laugh because she thinks she can learn, because she thinks that one day she'll be like the rest of them, talking seriously, confidently, with knowledge, livin' a civilized life. Well, she can't be like that really but bring her in because she's good for a laugh!

I'm all right with you, here in this room; but when I saw those people you were with I couldn't come in. I would have seized up. Because I'm a freak. I can't talk to the people I live with anymore. An' I can't talk to the likes of them on Saturday, or them out there, because I can't learn the language. I'm a half-caste. I went back to the pub where Denny was, an' me mother, an' our Sandra, an' her mates. I'd decided I wasn't comin' here again. I went into the pub an' they were singin', all of them singin' some song they'd learnt from the juke-box. An' I stood in that pub an' thought, just what the frig am I trying to do? Why don't I just pack it in an' stay with them, an' join in the singin'?

(Angrily.) You think I can, don't you? Just because you pass a pub doorway an' hear the singin' you think we're all O.K., that we're all survivin', with the spirit intact. Well I did join in with the singin', I didn't ask any questions, I just went along with it. But when I looked round me mother had stopped singin', an' she was cryin', but no one could get it out of her why she was cryin'. Everyone just said she was pissed an' we should get her home. So we did, an' on the way I asked her why. I said, 'Why are y' cryin', Mother?' She said, 'Because — because we could sing better songs than those.' Ten minutes later, Denny had her laughing and singing again, pretending she hadn't said it. But she had. And that's why I came back. And that's why I'm staying.

Katrina is one of three agoraphobic women who has been persuaded to take part in a jumble sale outside her home. She used to be a singer but now lives a sheltered life, completely protected by her overbearing husband Maurice. Katrina is conscious of her own good looks and has a sharp tongue towards the other women who are less 'feminine' in the accepted sense. In this speech she is describing her day to the trainee social worker, Fliss.

Bazaar And Rummage *by Sue Townsend*

Katrina   Well at eight o'clock Maurice brings me my breakfast on a tray. I have half a grapefruit, a soft-boiled egg, toast soldiers, a cup of tea and a five-milligram Librium. Then when he's gone to work I listen to Terry Wogan. He sometimes plays one of Barry's records but he can never pronounce his name properly, he calls him Harry Banilow. Sometimes I think Terry does it on purpose. Then what do I do? Yes, so I get up and have a Sainsbury's bubble bath. Then I get out, cream my knees and elbows. Immac under my arms, put all my make-up on and do my hair. Then of course I have to choose what to wear. Well time's getting on so I go downstairs, he's done all the housework but I have to water the plants. Then I sit and listen to Barry until Maurice comes home. (. . .) He's home at one o'clock. He has tomato soup and two slices of bread and I have a doughnut, a cup of coffee and a five-milligram Librium. No sooner that's done than he goes back to work and I have to have a sleep until he comes back at teatime. Then, while we eat our digestives Maurice tells me all the news; all about the riots and the muggings and the rapes and the old people being murdered *(More emotionally.)* and the blacks kidnapping white women and all the little kiddies that's molested by perverts and the animals that's tortured by teenagers and the multiple crashes on the motorways and how people have been trapped inside their cars and been burnt alive.

She continues more normally.

Well, when he's told me all the latest, I have a ten-milligram Librium and he cooks the dinner.

Pause.

Meat, two veg, gravy, tin of fruit and Dream Topping, let's say. Then Gwenda comes round and Maurice and her talk about how the country's going down the drain. Then it's cocoa, two Cadbury's Fingers, Mogadon and bed.

There is a long pause during which time a siren is heard.

Teendreams follows the lives of two women showing how their teenage idealism of the sixties is eroded by the experiences of being a wife, mother and teacher in the seventies.

Rosie, the less politically aware of the two, marries young. As she grows older she comes to resent her husband's repressive attitude towards her need for personal fulfilment. This speech is addressed to a chauvinistic male teacher whom she has just met at a friend's house.

Teendreams *by David Edgar and Susan Todd*

Rosie *(quietly)*   When I was nineteen, I was asked to this wedding. And at the reception afterwards, met Howard. We stood near each other, giggled at the speeches, drank the fizzy wine. And then he asked me to go out with him, and I said yes, so out we went, and then he asked, well, in a month or so, if I would be engaged to him, and I said yes, and so engaged we were, and then before I knew it I was being asked if I would love and honour and obey, and I said yes, and love and honour and obey I did, and shortly after that I must have stopped the pill, cos I had Damion and three years later I had Sophie, complications and my tubes tied up, and I do not recall, throughout that happy fairy tale, one single, solitary choice at all. I never chose to get engaged. Be married. Have my children. I was chosen. (. . .)

Now, you will know the concept of the Deja Vu. The feeling, I've done this, been here before. It's quite disturbing. Even more disturbing is the feeling that I had, from time to time, throughout my happy fairy life, a feeling in the night-time, in the darkness, of Non Deja Vu, a sense of loss of something that I should have been, but hadn't, sense of never really doing, never thinking, anything; a sense of being thought and being done. Which you will doubtless find it hard to understand. Because, although there's limits to your choices, you can choose and map your life. Whereas, my life, and Trisha's, and Denise's, aren't like yours, because they are not mappable. They're mapped.

So don't you talk to me, to Frances or to them, about free choice. Cos, on that score, dear Nick, you just don't know you're born.

Plenty offers a view of the post-war years through the eyes of Susan, who as a young girl worked in the French Resistance. She is a highly intelligent woman, cryptic and reserved. Susan has a strong destructive streak towards the men she knows but is supportive of her women friends and is constantly searching for the strength of value and purity of ideal that she felt during the war. This scene takes place just after the war. Susan is talking to her bohemian artist friend Alice.

Plenty *by David Hare*

Susan   Mr Medlicott has moved into my office. (...)

Or rather, more sinister still he has removed the frosted glass between our two offices. (...)

I came in one morning and found the partition had gone. I interpret it as the first step in a mating dance. I believe Medlicott stayed behind one night, set his ledger aside, ripped off his tweed suit and his high collar, stripped naked, took up an axe, swung it at the partition, dropped to the floor, rolled over in the broken glass till he bled, till his whole body streamed blood, then he cleared up, slipped home, came back next morning and waited to see if anything would be said. But I have said nothing. And neither has he. He puts his head down and does not lift it till lunch. I have to look across at his few strands of hair, like seaweed across his skull. And I am frightened of what the next step will be. (...)

The sexual pressure is becoming intolerable.

They smile.

One day there was a condom in his turn-up. Used or unused I couldn't say. But planted without a doubt. Again, nothing said. I tried to laugh it off to myself, pretended he'd been off with some whore in Limehouse and not bothered to take his trousers off, so that after the event the condom had just absent-mindedly fallen from its place and lodged alongside all the bus tickets and the tobacco and the Smarties and the paper-clips and all the rest of it. But I know the truth. It was step two. And the dance has barely begun.

Pause.

Alice. I must get out.

This play is set in Manchester and looks at the relationship of mother and daughter between four generations of women. Doris is the eldest of these women. This speech takes place at the end of the play, when Doris would have been about twenty-three years old. She has just returned from a picnic where her future husband has proposed to her. She is wearing a nineteen twenties' print dress, and is breathless with her hair awry. It is May 1923.

My Mother Said I Never Should
by Charlotte Keatley

Doris   Mother! Mother? Mother! Oh, what do you think! It's happened, happened to me! All the way back on the train I could hardly keep still, I don't know what the other passengers must've thought, but I wouldn't be ladylike. Mother! Come and look. Do I look different? I must look different, I feel as though I've swallowed a firework. Oh it was a lovely, lovely day. We took a picnic, climbed up to the Waterloo memorial, sat in the sunshine and it was after we'd finished the egg and cress; he couldn't wait till after the fruit cake! I felt so – shy, suddenly – I had to just stare and stare at the tablecloth while he was asking, blue and yellow squares, there was an ant struggling to carry a piece of cress across the corner. . . . These are things you remember all your life, I suppose. I didn't think it would be like this.

Pause.

And then we just ran and ran! Talked, made plans. I felt somehow – weedy!

Laughs.

– Sort of silly, for having given in . . . to – love! – Do you know what I mean?

Silence.

Mother? We ate your fruit cake on the train, Jack put a paper down so as not to drop crumbs on the velvet upholstery, but then he sat on a strawberry – and oh, I got a grass stain on my frock, but Jack says he'll buy me a new one. *And*, Mother, *and* I got promoted to Head of Infants this morning! Miss Butterworth called me into her office, my heart was in my mouth, I thought she was going to tick me off for this dress being too short! . . . Jack was very proud when I told him, but of course he says I shan't need to work when we're – when we're – oh, of course he's going to ask you first, he's waiting in the front room, I opened the curtains so the neighbours can see – Oh and –

Lights begin to fade.

I've seen just the posy, tiny white flowers, in the window of Ambleton's . . . Oh Mother, I'm so happy. SO HAPPY! I suppose, really and truly, this is the beginning of my life!

*Lights fade to a single spot on **Doris's** face, then snap out.*

A group of wives and mothers rally to the CND cause, demonstrating outside US air bases and helping the Greenham Common women. Their husbands are all members of the Territorial Army and refuse to take the women seriously. Eventually, in an attempt to force their men to take note of the anti-nuclear issue, the women go on sexual strike. This speech takes place three months into the strike. Eileen is beginning to voice some doubts about the strike to her friend, Norma, who is also on strike.

Not With A Bang *by Mike Harding*

Eileen   Well I don't know, it's getting me down a bit now this. I mean it's been three months. I never thought we'd last out. I mean I was never very physical, you know, didn't even like Postman's Knock when I was a kid or going on the hobby-horse in the playground, but I think I'm starting to feel a bit frustrated now. You know this morning I was reaching for something on the top shelf in the kitchen and as I was leaning up against the washing-machine it started going to spin dry and all the vibrations went through me and it got me – (. . .)

She stops.

Well I don't know how to say really, I mean, I thought, ooh that's nice and I just sort of stayed there and kept it on fast hot wash and spin. (. . .)

Well, then there was a knock at the door and I knew it was the Co-op dairy for his money, and well me legs were all shakin' and that and you know I told you about him, him with the red 'air and the moustache, the really 'andsome one that looks like Jess Conrad, you know the one that keeps smiling at me – he's just got divorced you know by the way. Well, I went to the door and I felt like I was in a dream, I was all twitchy and, and well, hot and shaky and I opened the door and, ooh I feel stupid. (. . .)

Well, it was the other one, his little bandy mate with the squint and no teeth, so I just burst out crying and said 'No yoghurt on Saturday' and ran back in.

Rose is a warm-hearted teacher who becomes frustrated at the state of her life, both professionally and emotionally. She seeks release through having an affair. Sally is Rose's friend, an exuberant, vivacious woman with a sardonic sense of humour. It is only in the presence of her lover that Sally reveals her tender, protective side. The speech takes place when Rose comes to visit Sally for a chat. They are soon immersed in their favourite subject – sexual encounters.

Rose *by Andrew Davies*

Sally   Saw one today, on me way home from the library. Just been giving me chat to the Friends of the Cotswold Countryside about the natural ecology of the English hedgerow. (. . .)

Oh yes, it had gone down a treat, and I was just strolling along, singing a merry song, as is my wont. And then this figure emerged from behind a tree, and adopted a significant pose. (. . .)

Ah. Well. I'm afraid I played my part badly in this encounter. Thing is, as you know, I can hardly see a thing without my specs, and I didn't have them on. So we both sort of stood there. . . . He didn't say anything and I didn't say anything. It seemed to be his move. Funny, I thought. Then I vaguely discerned there was something wrong with his kecks. Has he torn them on some barbed wire, I mused innocently. Is he in need of help? Do I look the sort of lady who carries a needle and thread about with her? So screwed up me eyes and me courage, and peered closer. And there it was. (. . .)

His compendium! (. . .)

Shimmering vaguely through the mist. Blimey, Sally, I thought. Had again! (. . .)

One of those really tricky problems in etiquette. I had me specs in me pockets, see. Should I put them on or not? If I did, would he be pleased at my friendly show of interest, or would he be goaded into savage animal lust and it's a long time since I've come across a bit of animal lust – or worst of all, would he think I was trying to make some sort of satirical point about the minuscule dimensions of his compendium? (. . .)

In the event, we both sort of stayed where we were, a sort of bucolic tableau, until finally he whisked back behind his tree and did a bit of grunting, and I went on me merry way.

Phil is one of four friends who all support Manchester United Football Club. **True, Dare, Kiss** is the second in a trilogy of plays which follow the fortunes of the girls from their late teens to their early twenties.

Phil has left Manchester to attend Bristol University. She is a highly intelligent, rather naïve girl who tends to denigrate her own background, feeling that it is somehow inadequate in comparison to those of her university friends. Here she is talking to her graduate student boyfriend, Nash, whom she regards as being incredibly cultured and in control of his life.

True, Dare, Kiss *by Debbie Horsfield*

Phil *(suddenly)* Look, there's no such place as Coronation Street.

Nash looks up, then goes back to his work.

They don't believe yer, do they? Where y'from, Phil? Manchester?
Never. Beer an' bingo? Tripe an' onions? Rovers Return? That's right.
Friday nights down the dog track – blow yer wages – batter the wife.
Education? What's the point, love? Yer only gonna get married.
Oh, we're all dead ignorant up North, aren't we?

Pause.

I am though, aren't I? It's dead embarrassing. How d'y'admit y've
never been wind-surfing – never read *Gormenghast* – never heard of
David Hockney? I've missed out. I'm not a Feminist, Friend-of-the-
Earth, Ban-the-Bomber, Real Ale Freak. What am I? I don't know
anything. Y'go to school, y'sit exams – nobody tells yer about Jean-Luc
Godard or reading the *Guardian*. Football? Oh but you don't actually
go? Oh no, not me. Not much. What d'y'do if y'can't stand yoga,
despise *The Hobbit* – an' thought that Donizetti was a cheap martini?
How can y'be taken seriously if yer favourite film's *The Jungle Book* (...)
It's not art, though, is it?

Four A Levels, eight O Levels – I come here an' I know sod-all. Okay,
okay, *you* say it doesn't matter. You say 'so what?' (...)

Did *you* think Eugene O'Neill played on the right wing for Northern
Ireland?

Summer shows the reunion of two women who were respectively servant and mistress in an occupied area of Europe during the war. The mistress collaborated but her collaboration saved the servant's life. In their meeting the past is searingly revived.

Marthe was the servant. A gracious woman who is dying of an incurable disease. She now lives in the old house of her mistress.

Summer *by Edward Bond*

Marthe *(working)*   What's more useless than death? Life without death would be. How could you find anything beautiful if you looked at it forever? You'd grow tired of it. Why fall in love if it lasted forever? When you'd forgiven yourselves a thousand times you'd tire of forgiveness. You'd grow tired of changing the people you loved.

Ann returns with three folded chairs, opens them and sets them at the table.

If you ate for eternity why bother to taste what you're eating? You can taste the next meal. When you've cried for one mistake you wouldn't cry for the next. You'd have eternity to put it right. Soon your eyes would be full of sleep. You'd go deaf. You wouldn't listen to voices because they would give you the trouble of answering. Why listen to them? It would be useless to know which was a sparrow or a waterfall. In eternity there would be no future. You'd sit on the ground and turn to stone. Dust would pile up and bury you. If we didn't die we'd live like the dead. Without death there's no life. No beauty, love or happiness. You can't laugh for more than a few hours or weep more than a few days. No one could bear more than one life. Only hell could be eternal. Sometimes life is cruel and death is sudden – that's the price we pay for not being stones. Don't let the lightning strike you or madmen burn your house. Don't give yourself to your enemies or neglect anyone in need. Fight. But in the end death is a friend who brings a gift: life. Not for you but the others. I die so that you might live. Did you call David? Breakfast's ready.

Chameleon shows how two black office workers combat the daily racism they encounter. Benjamin has assumed the attitudes and prejudices of his white boss in an attempt to further his career. Marcia finds this betrayal of his own colour both naïve and ignorant and in this speech attempts to raise Benjamin's black consciousness.

Chameleon *by Michael Ellis*

Marcia (*to***Benjamin**)   I remember in my last job there were these two Nigerian girls. I always used to think of African people as much more united than us West Indians or the Americans but they'd come in in the morning and by ten o'clock they'd be at one another's throats. No matter how far you set them apart their Black skins would draw them together and their Black skins would rip them apart. First there'd be the vocal friction and then the physical ignition. The white girls positively glowed at the flying insults about the other's natty hair, the Blackest skin or the men they'd been having and you know what I thought as I watched them, Benjamin? (. . .)

I thought they knew what they were doing, exactly what they were doing. They were aware of their entertainment value and they played it up. Each fight would, predictably, reveal a few more sordid details about their private lives, a little more hair would be torn out, a little more clothing would be ripped. They were only doing what was expected of them. If once they got together and chatted among themselves it was seen as conspiracy, the whites were excluded, we had to be planning some kind of plot to bring down the white power structure, we had to be talking revolution. No, it is not healthy! To this day I think those girls knew what they were doing as they spat in one another's eyes. And it worked, too. As far as I know they're still there getting regular wage rises with the supervisor . . . God, I hated that bitch; claiming there was equal opportunity for everyone in that office. I suppose she had a point, though. I've never met a white person yet who didn't show that integration meant whites policing Blacks as Blacks try to cut one another's throats. That's the real reason I hit her. I'd been planning to for a long time.

Spell #7 is written as a poetic piece reflecting the lives and experiences of black people in America. A group of performers meet in a bar to sing, dance and talk about their lives.

Natalie is a not very successful performer. She is astutely aware of the advantages of being white.

Spell #7 *by Ntozake Shange*

natalie   as a red-blooded white woman/ i cant allow you all to go on
like that

Natalie starts jocularly.

cuz today i'm gonna be a white girl/ i'll retroactively wake myself
up/ ah low & behold/ a white girl in my bed/ but first i'll haveta call a
white girl i know to have some more accurate information/ what's the
first thing white girls think in the morning/ do they get up being glad
they aint niggahs / do they remember mama/ or worry abt gettin to
work/ do they work?/ do they play isadora & wrap themselves in sheets
& go tip toeing to the kitchen to make maxwell house coffee/ oh I
know/ the first thing a white girl does in the morning is fling her hair/
   so now i'm done with that/ i'm gonna water my plants/ but am i a po
white trash white girl with a old jellyjar/ or am i a sophisticated &
protestant suburbanite with 2 valiums slugged awready & a porcelain
water carrier leading me up the stairs strewn with heads of dolls &
nasty smellin white husband person's underwear/ if i was really
protected from the niggahs/ i might go to early morning mass & pick
up a tomato pie on the way home/ so i cd eat it during the young & the
restless. in williams arizona as a white girl/ i cd push the navaho
women outta my way in the supermarket & push my nose in the air so i
wdnt haveta smell them. coming from bay ridge on the train i cd smile
at all the black & puerto rican people/ & hope they cant tell i want
them to go back where they came from/ or at least be invisible

The Normal Heart is about the growing danger of the AIDS crisis in New York. It shows the efforts of the gay community to gain recognition for the seriousness of the disease in the face of the indifference and prejudice of the authorities. Emma is one of the first doctors specializing in treatment of the disease. In this scene she has been called before a fund-donating board to plead for more money to help AIDS cases. She is increasingly frustrated at the lack of resources made available to her as the epidemic spreads. Emma is wheelchair-bound.

The Normal Heart *by Larry Kramer*

Emma Another idiot. And, by the way, a closeted homosexual who is doing everything in his power to sweep this under the rug, and I vowed I'd never say that in public. How does it always happen that all the idiots are always on your team? You guys have all the money, call the shots, shut everybody out, and then operate behind closed doors. I am taking care of more victims of this epidemic than anyone in the world. We have more accumulated test results, more data, more frozen blood samples, more experience! How can you not fund my research or invite me to participate in yours? A promising virus has already been discovered – in France. Why are we being told not to co-operate with the French? Why are you refusing to co-operate with the French? Just so you can steal a Nobel Prize? Your National Institutes of Health received my first request for research money two years ago. It took you one year just to print up application forms. It's taken you two and a half years from my first reported case just to show up here to take a look. The paltry amount of money you are making us beg for – from the four billion dollars you are given each and every year – won't come to anyone until only God knows when. Any way you add all this up, it is an unconscionable delay and has never, never existed in any other health emergency during this entire century. While something is being passed around that causes death. We are enduring an epidemic of death. Women have been discovered to have it in Africa – where it is clearly transmitted heterosexually. It is only a question of time. We could all be dead before you do anything. You want my patients? Take them! TAKE THEM!

She starts hurling her folders and papers at him, out into space.

Just do something for them! You're fucking right I'm imprecise and unfocused. And you are all idiots!

The Art Of Success is set in Hogarth's London where corruption, dissolution and disease are rife. Hogarth struggles to establish a copyright on his engravings but with little thought as to whether his subjects wish to have their image sold to the public.

Louisa is Hogarth's prostitute lover called upon to perform those services which he would never ask of his wife.

The Art Of Success *by Nick Dear*

Louisa *(shivers)*   Wind off the Thames blows down the avenues,
round the rotunda, through the triumphal arches and directly up my
skirt. I must have the coldest legs in England. A sailor in a Bermondsey
cellar said that in China they tell of a wind disease, a cold, cold wind
blowing round the body, typhoon in your arms and legs, whispering
draughts at the back of your skull. I told him I think I've got it, mate, it
all sounds dead familiar. He laughed and bit my nipple with
splintering teeth. What I would have loved, at that moment, what I
longed for, was that all the air would whoosh out of me like a burst
balloon, and I sink down to nothing at his feet, and teach the
disbelieving rat a lesson. Here I am out in all weathers, all the
entrances and exits in my body open to the elements day and freezing
night, what's to stop the gale when it comes in and fills me? And blows
round my bones for ever? – Wait, is he walking this way? That
dragoon? He looks so sad . . . doesn't he look sad . . . I don't know, they
call this place a pleasure garden, I've never seen such misery, I'd
christen it the garden of wind and disappointment, or cold and frosted
cunt.

Jane has entered, unseen. She listens.

Is he coming over here? Come along, then, miss, get all your gusts and
breezes together. . . . Nice time with an old windbag, soldier? It's not
wearing any knickers.

Great Celestial Cow is about the lives of Asian women in England and the difficulties they face through racial prejudice and cultural difference. Rose is a white, working-class native of Leicester. She befriends Sita who has recently arrived from India. This speech is a monologue to a prospective buyer for her mail order catalogue. It takes place in Rose's living-room with loud reggae music playing in the background.

The Great Celestial Cow *by Sue Townsend*

Rose *(off)*   Delroy! Delroy! Turn that bleddy music down! *Delroy*!!!
I've gorra customer with me!

Sorry to keep you waiting – I'll be out in a bit – I'm just putting me
face on. Ooh, it's like plastering a wall – Max Factor oughta present me
with a long service medal.

Rose rushes on.

Right, this is me spring catalogue. We'll have a good look through it in
a bit. But I can recommend it. If it weren't for this, me and Delroy'd be
going round naked. I mean, who can afford to pay cash for new stuff
nowadays? I never thought I'd gerrit going. When I seen the Indians
moving in round here I thought, oh well, you can say goodbye to
building yourself a round up, Rose. I were a bit suspicious of 'em at
first. Well, when they first come, some of 'em looked at me like I were
muck. I know I ain't much, but I ain't muck. You can get used to owt
can't you? And some of them are really nice – not all, but some. Any
road up, as it turned out, I've got myself a nice little round going in our
street. I take me catalogue round of a Wednesday, collect the money,
and after we've had a few drinks, I ask 'em if they want owt else. Sita's
paying me one-fifty a week for some sheets she had last year. When
she's finished paying, she's having a ottoman to put 'em in.

Bibi had her first pair of jeans from out my club – Christ, didn't that
cause a stink! You'd have thought she'd had a G-string or sommat!
Them two old bags, bleddy Dadima an' Masi, wanted Sita to send 'em
back, but Sita stuck to her guns. O' course, that were a few years ago –
she's having a bit of a wobbler now. I don't know what's up, but
sommat is. She's not the same girl as come here eight years ago. To tell
the truth, I don't know her now. She works too hard. She's out the
house at eight, and don't get back till after six, and I know she don't sit
down when she gets home. She's always up and doing – has to be busy.
Now I've learnt the secret of relaxation? I take life gradual, have a few
laughs. It's laughing's kept me going. An' it's free, so I can recommend
that and all! Anyway, what you going to have?

Up To You, Porky is a compilation of comedy sketches and monologues. This speech has no specific context and is entirely open to interpretation by the actor.

Up To You, ~~~~~~~~~~~~~~~~

Guide   Right, I'm your official guide. Now before I show you round, I'll just fill you in on a few details, as we call them. As you can see, we're standing in the hall of the Haworth Parsonage, where Haworth's parson, the Reverend Brontë, lived here with his daughters, the famous Brontë sisters, now, alas, no longer with us – but they have left us their novels, which I've not read, being more of a Dick Francis nut. Now, if you pass by me into the parlour (mind my vaccination) . . . This is what was known in those days as a parlour, somewhat similar to our lounge-type sitting-room affair in modern technology. I'm afraid the wallpaper isn't the original period to which we're referring to, it is actually Laura Ashley, but I think it does give some idea of what life must have been like in a blustery old Yorkshire community of long ago.

That portrait on the wall is actually of Charlotte Brontë, one of the famous Brontë sisters, and of course to us she may seem a rather gloomy-looking individual; but you must remember these days she'd have a perm or blusher, or I suppose even drugs would have helped her maintain a more cheerful attitude. In fact, she'd probably not be dead if she was alive today. Now if you'd like to hutch through to the Reverend Brontë's study. . . . This is a typical study in which to do studying – as you can see there's a table, chair . . . (oh my poncho, I've been looking for that . . .) and I like to imagine this elderly old gentleman hunched over a sermon, probably thinking, 'Where's my cocoa, I suppose those darn girls are in the middle of another chapter,' or something like that he may have been thinking – we just can't be sure . . . Of course he died eventually, unfortunately. You must remember this is an extremely exposed part of the United Kingdom, I mean, it's May now, and I'm still having to slip that polo-neck under my bolero.

Our Country's Good takes as its basis the performance of Farquhar's *The Recruiting Officer* by a cast of convicts in Australia in 1789.

Liz, an angry and unpenitent convict, is playing the part of Melinda. She is suspected of having taken part in a raid on the stores and has been sentenced to be hanged. In this speech she talks for the first time about her past and why she is in a penal colony. Like her fellow convicts she is in chains.

Our Country's Good
by Timberlake Wertenbaker

Liz   Luck? Don't know the word. Shifts its bob when I comes near.
Born under a ha'penny planet I was. Dad: he was a nibbler, don't want
to get crapped. Mum leaves, wants the water of life. Five brothers, I'm
the only titter. I takes in washing. Then. My own father. Lady's
walking down the street, takes her wiper. She screams, he's
shoulder-clapped, says, it's not me, Sir, it's Lizzie, look, she took it. I'm
stripped, beaten in the street, everyone watching. That night, I take my
dad's cudgel and try to kill him, I prig all his clothes and go to my older
brother. He don't want me, another tooth. Liz, he says, why trine for a
make, when you can wap for a winne. I'm no dimber mort, I says.
Don't ask you to be a swell mollisher, Sister, coves want Miss Laycock,
don't look at your mug. So I begin to sell my mother of saints. I thinks
I'm in luck when I meet the swell cove. He's a bobcull. He says to me,
it's not enough to sell your mossie face, Lizzie, it don't bring no shiners
no more. Shows me how to spice the swells. So. Swell has me up the
wall, flashes a rum thimble, I lifts it. But one time I stir my stumps too
slow, the swell squeaks beef, the snoozie hears, I'm nibbed. It's up the
ladder to rest, I thinks when I goes up before the fortune teller, but no,
the judge's a bobcull, I nap the King's pardon and it's seven years
across the herring pond. Jesus Christ the hunger on the ship, sea crabs
won't touch me no rantum scantum, no food, but here, the Governor
says, new life, you could nob it here, Lizzie, I think, bobcull gov, this
niffynaffy play, not too much work, good crew of rufflers, Kable,
Arscott, but no, Ross don't like my mug, I'm nibbed again and now it's
up the ladder to rest for good. Well. Lizzie Morden's life. And you,
Wisehammer, how did you get here?

When I Was A Girl ... is set in two time periods showing Fiona and Vari, as grown women and as teenagers, coming to sexual awareness in nineteen-fifties Scotland.

Fiona, caught in a love-hate battle with her mother, becomes pregnant at the age of sixteen. She does this as a means of preventing her mother's remarriage. She then regrets her action and attempts to strike a number of bargains with God – good deeds in return for no baby. This speech is one of Fiona's attempts to impress God with the number of charitable actions she has performed. It takes place on a beach in 1966.

When I Was A Girl I Used To Scream And Shout *by Sharman MacDonald*

Fiona *(very quickly)*   Last week, I was on the bus, upstairs. I was going to see Dorothy and this girl up the front, she started having a fit or something. Must have been the heat. There were lots of people there between her and me but they, none of them . . . I went over to her and did what I could. She was heavy. I'd heard about them biting through their tongues. Epileptics. It wasn't pretty. Me and this other bloke took her to the hospital. But I saw her first. He wouldn't have done anything if I hadn't. I didn't get to see Dorothy. Well? That's worth something, isn't it? God. Are you listening? I'm not trying to bribe you. It's plain economics. I mean, I've made a mistake. It was my fault and I was wrong. I take it all on me. OK. Now if you let it make me pregnant . . . God. Listen, will you. If I'm pregnant it'll ruin four people's lives. Five. Right? My mum'll be disappointed and her man'll walk out on her. That's two. Are you with me, God? I'll not be very happy. My mother'll hate me for the rest of my life for what I've done and that's not easy to live with. That's three. I'm still counting, God. Ewan'll be in for it. Well, he can't avoid it. I'm illegal and I've never been out with anybody else. Not that nobody fancied me. I wouldn't like you to think I was unpopular. Lots of people fancied me. My mum said I had to wait till I was sixteen. Then she relented just when Ewan happened to be there. Poor old Ewan. That's four, God, that's four. Then there's the baby. If it's there and if I have it it's got no chance. It would be born in Scotland. Still there, are you? I hate Scotland. I mean, look at me. If I have an abortion the baby'll be dead so that'll be five anyway.

Great Celestial Cow is about the lives of Asian women in England and the difficulties they have to face through racial prejudice and cultural difference. Bibi is a westernized girl of eighteen. She finds it hard to reconcile her education with the submissive role she is expected to take as a daughter and prospective wife. In this speech Bibi is talking directly to the audience, having sneaked out for a night's dancing. It is set in the loo in the Palais, at midnight.

The Great Celestial Cow *by Sue Townsend*

Bibi   Well, I had a brilliant time tonight. Debauchery galore there was. I've been with every bloke in the Palais – must be 200. I came in at eight and it's Cinderella time now. So it's not bad going is it? It's my legs you see. One glimpse and the English blokes are sitting on their haunches panting for it and I'm so depraved and corrupted by the West that I let them have it. You see I've no morality of my own. No respect for my body. I've got three 'A' levels but no intelligence. I can't be trusted, after all I'm only twenty. Mum knows I come here. There's nothing I wouldn't tell her – well the odd thing. But Mum doesn't count for much in our family. When it's not at Sketchleys I keep me gear in a black plastic bag in Mum's wardrobe, next to her bucket. It's pathetic. Here I am an Asian girl caught in a culture clash. See these things each side of my head? Inverted commas. Now the English *are* lucky – they don't have family problems.

No, they sit around in shafts of sunlight eating cornflakes, then get up and run around meadows in slow motion. One in four that is. The other three are undergoing divorce or family therapy. Yes we all jostle for space on the *Guardian* Women's Page. There's me, cheek by jowl with 'Shall I, a committed Socialist, send my Rupert to public school?' Now that *would* make you toss and turn at night. I'm educated. I'm healthy, and I'll make myself some sort of life. But until then I'll change in the bog. Me mum's got enough on her plate.

Pause.

If anyone asks, I've been babysitting.

Adult Child/Dead Child follows the life of a disturbed and abused child as it grows up and attempts to come to terms with the world. It is a one-person show.

Adult Child/Dead Child *by Claire Dowie*

My father was an actor
professional pretender
pretended to be a father

pretended to have feelings
pretended enthusiasm
demanded perfection
demanded perfection
100% do it right, do it the best
be brainy, be sporty, be talented, be good
academic athlete
well mannered, polite, know it all, do it all
100% do it right, do it the best
I cried, I would cry
I would cry & I failed
always failed
for my professional pretending father
& his daughter, the apple of his eye
who could do no wrong.

I remember being in the garden of our old house, I was about six or
seven & there were friends of my parents visiting. I can't remember
now who, but somebody gave me a cowboy & indian set. This was a
cowboy hat & gun & holster & a tin star with the word 'sheriff' on it &
an indian feather thing with a band on it for a hat & a tomahawk & my
dad said let's play with it & first he was the cowboy & I was the indian
& everybody was watching & I ran at him with my tomahawk but he
shot me so I lost & then we changed round & I was the cowboy & my
dad was the indian but before I could shoot him he threw the
tomahawk & it hit my head & he said it was Custer's last stand &
everybody laughed (I thought he said 'custard' & I didn't understand)
& he said I was hopeless because I died twice & I didn't want to play
with my cowboy & indian set anymore but later on that night I decided
to be the indian & sneak up on him quietly but when I sneaked into
their bedroom & jumped on him with my tomahawk he woke up.
Didn't act like a cowboy, acted like an angry father.

A young girl returns to her childhood holiday home to recuperate after an illness. She finds herself haunted by a spirit which terrifies her and propels her into a state of continual movement.

The psychiatrist is brought in to treat her. Although originally cynical about her patient, she gradually comprehends the depth of fear which Kay is feeling and begins to doubt her own professional ability for the first time.

Fugue *by Rona Munro*

Psychiatrist She was my first solo case. Before that it had been so
easy, school, exams: endless pens dancing over endless blank sheets to
the accompaniment of approving ticks in the margin. It was all a
wonderful game with just enough challenge to give easy win after easy
win a real sparkle. I've always run at things early, jumped fences I
wasn't grown for. I used to think I was going to be a child prodigy once
. . . well I grew up, so I blew that one . . . but fully qualified and
practising psychiatry at twenty-five? Oh that's a triumph, that's a real
lie awake, count your blessings and smirk in nauseating self
congratulation that one. I was a success story. . . . That's what made
all this such a shock, the amazement, the horrified amazement I felt
looking at this unexpected body lying across my path, glaring balefully
at me, waiting to bite my feet when I tried to jump over her . . .

I didn't know what was wrong with her. I didn't know how to begin. At
first I thought she was a bit of a fake, a melodrama addict. The way she
sat, held her head, everything screamed . . . 'I have been through a
terrible ordeal, I've touched life at its raw core, gazed on demons and
now I suffer for it.'

Hand on brow.

but then . . . I saw that underneath the prickles she was *so* scared and
she was trying to hide it . . . that's what this dumb with suffering bit
was all about. She was trying to play it down.

Then I thought: Maybe I'll botch this. Maybe in the glare of a
thousand flashbulbs poised to capture my learned and precocious
conclusions for the nation's press, I'm going to fall flat on my face. And
for the first time in my life I really believed that *I* could fail. Not as an
idea that gave the edge to some heady gambling with life but as a *fact*. I
wasn't in control. *I* was terrified.

All that came out were the stiff formal catch phrases, copybook
questions that built a wall between us.

Messiah is set in seventeenth-century Poland. The Jews, having suffered barbaric slaughter at the hands of the Cossacks, become obsessed with the idea of the imminent arrival of the Messiah and a religious fervour sweeps through the Jewish community.

Rachel is in her late twenties. A plain woman with buck teeth and pock-marked skin, she has been talked into an arranged marriage with an older man whom she dislikes. She talks continually to God in long monologues, hoping to gain some proof of his existence.

Rachel falls in love with Asher, her nephew by marriage. When Asher removes his shirt in front of her Rachel rushes to talk to God, having never seen a man's body uncovered before.

Messiah *by Martin Sherman*

Rachel   Blessed God, we have to talk. I was angry at you, I wasn't
going to speak to you ever again, but we *have to talk*! I've never seen a
man's body before. Reb Ellis never undresses in front of me. And when
he comes into bed, it must always be dark. Well, those are *your* laws. Or
at least laws made in your name – some day we have to discuss that.
But with Reb Ellis, believe me, your laws are fine. You must have made
them because you knew so many women marry fat, ugly men. But
suppose a woman marries an Asher? Then what an awful law! Oh
Lord, do you realize a man's chest can be beautiful, not just his face?
And perhaps a woman's chest too. . . . To a man. My breasts. . . . Did
you ever think about that? My breasts may be very nice. So if that's the
case why can't I wear clothes around my face and leave my breasts
bare?

Pause.

I'm having impure thoughts. Oh, am I having impure thoughts. He
asked me what I was thinking. How could I tell him? He'd run out and
find me a nettle. But he is so beautiful that now I want to believe in his
Messiah. And that's not right. One thing shouldn't mix itself up with
the other. Why do you make everything so confusing?

Pause.

I'm sorry. Forgive me for the things I say. I love you. You saved me
from the Cossacks. You do care. I know that. You're just quiet. Like
Mama.

Pause.

I haven't really seen a man's body. Only *half* a man's body.

Silence.

Only half.

Bazaar And Rummage is a comedy set in a church hall where a jumble sale is being held by a trainee social worker, three agoraphobics and Gwenda, an ex-agoraphobic and volunteer social worker.

Gwenda acts as a lifeline for the three women. As the women become more confident of being out in the world, Gwenda starts to feel threatened by their independence and becomes increasingly emotional. Here Gwenda is talking to the trainee social worker, Fliss, whilst unpacking boxes of jumble.

Bazaar And Rummage *by Sue Townsend*

Gwenda *(unaware that **Fliss** has gone, she continues stacking the books into paperback and hardback piles)*   I read a lot when I was a girl. Asthmatics are usually well read, have you noticed? I had Enid Blyton's complete works. Complete. My father brought one home every Friday night without fail. My mother had a quarter pound of Mint Imperials, father had two ounces of Shag and I had my new Enid Blyton. I'm sure that's why I'm quite without racial prejudice you know. Golly, Wog and Nigger were always my favourites, they were naughty to the other toys, but they always took their punishment well.

She finds Black Beauty.

Black Beauty! I could go on *Mastermind* with *Black Beauty* as my main subject.

Quickly.

What was Black Beauty's mother's name?

Carefully.

Duchess.

Quickly.

Who was the first man to break Black Beauty in?

Carefully.

Squire Gordon.

Quickly.

What lesson did Squire Gordon teach Black Beauty?

Softly.

You must never start at what you see, nor bite nor kick, nor have any will of your own. But always do your master's will, even though you may be very tired or hungry. That was more or less what father taught me. It's kept me in good stead, service first self second.

Rosy is one of four wives whose husbands are involved in a dubious business venture. The women have been instructed to meet for a celebratory dinner to be joined later by their menfolk – however, during dinner they receive an urgent call from their husbands to flee the country . . .

Rosy is the youngest and most innocent of the four and is quite overawed by the palatial home of her husband's partner, which she is visiting for the first time. Here she is talking to the partner's wife who takes no notice of her.

Made In Spain *by Tony Grounds*

Rosy   Oh, happy birthday. Anyway. I'm twenty years old. I used to be a hairdresser. Well, I am a hairdresser really. I'm just in between appointments, as they say. Still, I'm looking around. Nice break though. All day over hot heads, you know. And I'm married to Ray. And I love him. He's lovely to me. When I'm working, he phones me up every day at the salon. And says, 'All right, darling?' And I say, 'Yeah, I'm all right, Ray.' It's really embarrassing, because everyone looks and everyone's listening. He always asks me if I've made many mistakes. And generally I have. I think that's why I don't get as many appointments as the other girls. But I think one day we're going to be rich. Ray seems to be doing lots of deals at the moment. But I don't mind. He keeps saying, 'I'm going to see a man about a dog, babes.' I thought he meant it at first. I thought, 'What's he want with a dog?' I thought. Anyway my Ray's a street trader. He sells Pierre Cardin socks. Gets them off the back of a lorry and sells them cheap. Well everyone goes, 'Oh God, ain't they cheap?' And they're not, see. I've got a boy and he's two years old. Ray's mum looks after him quite a lot. Got no bloody choice there. 'Oh, I'll look after him,' she goes, 'I'll look after him. Oh, ain't he lovely?' I hate his mum! I really hate his mum! I think she quite likes me though, which makes me feel guilty. Anyway, Ray's lovely. He's twenty-eight. I love him. Especially in his big leather coat. He's really good-looking and all the girls look at him when he walks down the road and that. When I first saw him, I thought, I want that man. And I got him, somehow. In a disco . . . I just went up to him and went, 'Ain't your hair lovely?' And touched it. He seemed to get the message. Things started from there really. He keeps saying to me, 'I'm going to buy you your own business one day, babes.' Nice innit? I love my boy. Little Ray. He can't talk at the moment but he's cuddly and got fat legs. Ray keeps saying to him, 'You're going to be a footballer one day, aren't you going to be a footballer, little Ray?' And he goes . . .

Rosy pulls a gormless baby-face.

He doesn't know, you see. He doesn't know what it means.

Rosy looks around her. After a moment's thought, she nips across and lies on the sunbed. In her posh accent she calls 'waiter'. Then in mock American:

J.R. get out of my house!

This is the life. I've always been a hairdresser. I knew when I was at school I thought, 'Oh sod this.' As far as education is concerned, see, what does it mean? O levels and those other things, those degrees and things. No. I don't think you need them. I knew when I was fourteen I was going to be a hairdresser. Before that, I wanted to be a psychiatrist. Because I like the idea of a lovely wooden office. With a nice big desk, and lots of pens and that. And talking to people and saying, 'It's all right. You're a bit strained at the moment and your mind's a bit mad. But you're going to be all right, cos I'm going to look after you.' And, you know, they'd tell me all their problems and everything would be all right. But then I realized I wouldn't be able to do that cos you have to do lots and lots of studying. So I left school and got married to Ray when I was about seventeen. I met him when I was fourteen. At that disco I was telling you about. I was a virgin when I met Ray. Least that's what I told him. Don't say nuffin. You don't like to hurt their feelings. Least I don't.

A young female factory worker oversleeps and frantically tries to prepare herself and her baby for the forthcoming day – just as she is ready to leave she realizes she has lost her housekeys. In an attempt to retrace her steps she re-enacts the events of the previous evening. At this point she has just reached the stage of reliving the row she had with her husband. The play is a one-woman show.

Waking Up *by Dario Fo and Franca Rame*

She mimes turning on him in a rage.

Wife 'Listen, Stupid,' I tell him, 'I don't need to listen to feminists or radicals or anybody else to find out what a shitty life we lead. We both work like dogs and we never have a minute to talk. We never talk to each other! Is that marriage? Like does it ever even enter your mind to think about what's going on inside me? How I feel? Ever ask me if I'm tired . . . if you could give me a hand? Ha!'

Mimes bearing down on him threateningly.

'Who does the cooking? Me! Who does the washing up? Me! Who does the shopping? Me! And who does the death-defying financial acrobatics so we can get through to the end of the month? Me me me! And I'm working full time at the factory, remember. Your dirty socks . . . who washes them eh? How many times have you washed my socks? We should talk to each other, Luigi! We never talk. I mean it's okay with me that your problems are my problems but why can't my problems be your problems too instead of yours being ours and mine being only mine. I just want us to live together . . . not just in the same place. We should talk to each other! But what do we do? You come home from work, watch the telly and go to bed. Day after day it's always the same. Oh, except for Sundays.'

Scornfully.

'Hooray hooray it's football day! Every Sunday off you go to watch twenty-two idiots in their underpants kicking a ball around and some other mentally deficient maniac dashing up and down blowing a whistle!' He . . . that Luigi . . . he went purple in the face! You'd think I'd insulted his mother. 'How could a person like *you* ever know the first thing about sport?'

Brief pause.

Not the best thing he could've said, really.

With relish.

I freaked. 'Who the fuck would want to?' I shouted at him. And then I really started raving on like a lunatic. Oh I said it all. Everything! I screamed at him, he yelled back at me, I screamed louder, he yelled louder . . . we were just about shouting the building down. So finally I said 'Right! If this is marriage we've made a mistake!' And I picked up my mistake and I walked out.

The Accrington Pals are a battalion of men from Lancashire who are going over to fight in the trenches in the First World War. The play is about the women who are left behind, their growing independence as they take men's jobs, and their growing frustration at the censorship surrounding the fate of the 'Pals'.

May is in her late twenties, a forceful, seemingly bad-tempered and dragonish stall-holder. She loves her younger cousin, Tom, whom she looked after as a boy, but is embarrassed by her sexual desire for him and is unable to reveal the true nature of her feelings. Here she is talking to her lodger and friend, Eva, about the war and its possible duration.

The Accrington Pals *by Peter Whelan*

May   Not to take Tom and Ralph, no. Just long enough so's I can
afford the stock. We'll be singing round the piano yet. Round here they
think I'm queer in the head having a piano. But I could never let it go.
It was my father's. When I was small we were quite up in the world.
Lower-middle class. My father used to say upper-working but mother
said lower-middle. We lived in one of those villas in Hendal Street . . .
before it went downhill. But then father got this notion of speculating in
second-hand pianos and that was his undoing. Lost money on them.
Lost his job at Paxton's through slipping out to do deals. Did all kinds
of jobs after that. Oh he was a character! He once worked for a
photographer's shop. Now lots of people who had photos taken never
paid up. So, one week while father was in charge of the shop he put all
these people's photos in the window with the backs turned to the street
so you couldn't see the faces and a notice saying if they didn't pay up by
Saturday the photos would be turned round. Sparks flew then! He got
the sack. But then my mother, who was a very simple soul, and danced
attendance on him, morning, noon and night . . . well when she died it
seemed she'd secretly managed to scrimp and save a bit of money and it
looked like father and me might get a shop . . . a piano shop. But he
frittered most of it away. Then he rented the stall like I told you. Took
me from the mill to help run it. He just wouldn't do that kind of work.
Went into a depression. I ended up keeping him till he died. You won't
pass any of this on, will you?'

Joyriders is set in Belfast where a group of young offenders are taking part in a government Youth Opportunities Programme scheme. The aim of the scheme is to provide them with 'helpful' skills, enabling them to find employment at the end of the year. The young people, however, are less optimistic about their futures.

Sandra is a cynical, abrasive seventeen-year-old. She copes with her situation by maintaining her defences and rarely, if ever, revealing her true feelings. In this speech she has just been proposed to by Arthur, a fellow YOP schemer.

Joyriders *by Christina Reid*

Sandra The one an' only time I ever wore a white lace frock, Arthur, was for my first communion . . . an' my mother parades me down the road to get my photo tuk, an' she says to the photographer, 'Isn't our Sandra a picture? Won't she make a beautiful bride?' an' I told her I was never gonna get married, an' she got all dewy-eyed because she thought I wanted to be a nun. . . . A bride of Christ, or forty years' hard labour . . . my mother thinks anything in between is a mortal sin. . . . She married a big child like you, Arthur, an' what did it get her . . . eight kids an' twenty years' cookin', cleanin' an' survivin' on grants an' handouts. . . . You're too like my da fer comfort. Fulla big plans that'll come to nuthin' because yer too soft an' yer too easy-goin' an' havin' all that money won't make ye any different. Whatever your da an' the rest of your ones don't steal from ye, the world will. They'll ate ye alive. . . . You know what the big trick in this life is? It's knowin' what ye don't want, an' I don't want to be a back-seat joyrider, content to sit and giggle behind the fellas who do the stealin' an' the drivin' . . . I stole a car once . . . all by myself . . . I never told nobody, doin' it was enough . . . I just drove it roun' them posh streets in South Belfast until it ran outa petrol, an' then I walked home. Didn't need to boast about it the way the fellas do . . . just doin' it was enough. . . . When the careers' officer come to our school, he asked me what I wanted to do, an' I says, 'I wanna drive roun' in a big car like yer woman outa Bonnie and Clyde, an' rob banks,' an' he thought I was takin' a hand out him, so I says, 'All right then, I'll settle fer bein' a racin' driver.' An' he says, 'I'd advise you to settle for something less fantastic, Sandra.' . . . They're all the same. They ask ye what ye wanta be, an' then they tell ye what yer allowed to be. . . . Me wantin' to be a racin' driver is no more fantastical than Maureen believin' the fairy stories . . . dilly day-dream, just like her mother before her . . . somewhere over the rainbow, bluebirds die . . .

A group of five travellers come to Bangkok for a mixed trip of business and pleasure – for most of them the pleasure is of a sexual and exploitative nature. Frances, the only woman of the party, is unhappily married to Stephen. She is an intelligent, gentle woman gradually becoming more aware of her unhappiness both in her work and her marriage. In this scene she is talking to her lover, the only other member of the group to whom she can communicate.

Made In Bangkok *by Anthony Minghella*

Frances   No, not because of Stephen. I used to listen to this couple above me, at night – I'm talking about in London, years ago – and they used to have sex all the time. Great long loud sessions, really long and really loud and I used to lie in the dark and strain to listen, to hear them, screw up my eyes to catch the whole performance and imagine it: and my face used to go so hot . . . I remember that sensation: the sense of my face going hot, and straining to hear and these great groans and gasps and cries. You'd see them in the day time – this girl was perfectly ordinary, honestly, you wouldn't have given her a second look . . . a quiet hello, she'd be gone, and I'd know she has these fantastic orgasms. And I remember waking up one night and – being woken by this familiar noise – and straining to hear and my face going hot and then realizing it wasn't them, it was a baby, it was a baby half crying and it was Christopher, my son, and we weren't even in the same flat any more by this time and I'd woken, hardly woken, and made myself come to the sound of my son crying, waiting for me to feed him. I've been staring at the pool and it's black and I've been trying to remember that room, what it looked like: the room underneath the couple. And I can't. Where does it belong, our fantasy world? Do you know?

Three women factory workers in Manchester are made redundant just before Christmas. Lynda, the youngest of the three, persuades the other two to come down to London in order to make some Christmas money by working as prostitutes. She quickly breaks into the big time as a call-girl and begins to leave all trace of her working-class background behind. Here she is talking directly to the audience. She is wearing another expensive evening gown, an even more up-to-date hair-do and professional make-up. She looks ten years older than she did at the start of the play, with the beginnings of a new voice.

Thatcher's Women *by Kay Adshead*

Lynda   In the not too distant future I'd like to buy somewhere . . . a small studio flat to start with . . . somewhere nice . . . ish . . . Putney maybe or Primrose Hill and then a house outside London and a bigger luxury flat in the West End, for business purposes only. I'd like a Porsche and two holidays a year . . . Barbados and . . . Rome . . . possibly – oh, and a couple of fur coats.

At the moment most of my capital is having to be reinvested – my wardrobe, hairdressers, make-up, taxis, jewellery . . . elocution lessons . . . but if I can carry on my present earning capacity, it won't be long before I've covered overheads and I hit *pure profit*.

I'm a hard worker. I'm not supporting a habit, or . . . a pimp. I won't get pregnant.

In years to come I'll register myself as a small business . . . a little office somewhere . . . find a catchy title . . . 'Escort Elite' . . . get a few names and addresses on my books, boys as well as girls . . . only the best types . . . you know, educated, and well spoken . . .

Ecstatically.

I'll pay tax.

Don't get me wrong. I've every sympathy with women like Norah and Marje, but I can't help thinking they bring a lot on themselves. I dragged myself up from the gutter – why can't they?

Nicola is a shy and inarticulate sixteen-year-old girl living in Leicester. She has potentially a great deal of violence within her. She enters a local radio contest run by Leonard Brazil, the disc jockey. He becomes fascinated by Nicola and contrives for her to win through to the final heat of the competition. In this speech she has been asked by the radio presenter to describe her feelings while at a pop concert.

City Sugar *by Stephen Poliakoff*

Nicola   Oh . . . and . . .

Lost for words, she is extremely nervous.

– and then we went inside . . and the concert . . . and it was them of
course, and it was, you know . . . well it was all squashed – and some
people rushed up and fought to get close – and there was a bit of biting,
and that sort of thing, when they called out to us; they seemed a long
way off – a very long way away, in their yellow and everything. They
weren't loud – but they made you feel – I felt something come up, you
know, a little sort of . . .

A second of slight clenched feeling.

I got, you know, a bit worked up inside . . . they were moving very
slowly on stage like they'd been slowed down, made me feel strange –
then they held things up, waved it at us, smiling and everything, they
waved yellow scarves, Ross had a bit of yellow string he waved, I think
it was, a bit of yellow rope, and I half wanted to kick the girl in front of
me or something because I couldn't see; all the way through I had to
look at her great back, pressed right up against it. I remember I half
wanted to *get at it*. Move it. And I nearly dropped a ring.

She pulls at her finger.

I'd been pulling at, put it on specially.

Very nervous, she smiles.

If you drop anything it's gone for ever you know – can't bend down if
you're standing –

Smiles.

and if you drop yourself . . . then you'd be gone. When you rush out at
the end, you can see all the millions of things that have been dropped
shining all over the floor, nobody gets a chance to pick them up. And
then it was finished – you know, the concert, and I came outside. It was
cold, I was feeling a bit funny. Just walked along out there and I
thought maybe I was bleeding. I looked but I wasn't. Some people like
to be after a concert . . . but I wasn't.

The 'serious money' of the title refers to the fortunes to be made and lost working in the City on the Stock Exchange. Scilla's brother, a suspected insider dealer, has been murdered and she is attempting to find who the murderer is – though not for any reason of filial affection. The play is written as a modern verse play in which every character's over-riding passion is for money. This is a direct monologue to the audience.

Serious Money *by Caryl Churchill*

Scilla So Zac went back to Corman and I thought I'd better go to
work despite Jake being dead because Chicago comes in at one twenty
and I hate to miss it. I work on the floor of LIFFE, the London
International Financial Futures Exchange.

Trading options and futures look tricky if you don't understand it.
But if you're good at market timing you can make out like a bandit.
    (It's the most fun I've had since playing cops and robbers with
    Jake when we were children.)
A simple way of looking at futures is take a commodity,
Coffee, cocoa, sugar, zinc, pork bellies, copper, aluminium, oil –
    I always think pork bellies is an oddity.
    (They could just as well have a future in chicken wings.)
Suppose you're a coffee trader and there's a drought in Brazil like
    last year or suppose there's a good harvest, either way you might lose
    out
So you can buy a futures contract that works in the opposite direction
    so you're covered against loss, and that's what futures are basically
    about.
But of course you don't have to take delivery of anything at all.
You can buy and sell futures contracts without any danger of ending up
    with ten tons of pork bellies in the hall.

On the floor of LIFFE the commodity is money.
You can buy and sell money, you can buy and sell absence of money,
    debt, which used to strike me as funny.

For some it's hedging, for most it's speculation.
In New York they've just introduced a futures contract in inflation.
    (Pity it's not Bolivian inflation, which hit forty thousand per cent.)

I was terrified when I started because there aren't many girls and they
    line up to watch you walk,
And every time I opened my mouth I felt self-conscious because of the
    way I talk.
I found O levels weren't much use, the best qualified people are street
    traders.
But I love it because it's like playing a cross between roulette and space
    invaders.

Peggy is an American actress staying in the same hotel in India as a number of conference delegates. The conference is on poverty. Two of the delegates are attracted to her and she proposes a philosophical debate between the two of them – the winner to gain Peggy as a bedfellow.

She has already become involved with one and it is to him that she addresses the following speech.

Map Of The World *by David Hare*

Peggy   But the game was fun. No question. Great nights. What are
those things called? 'Angel Bars' we ate. Gloppy cherries covered in
chocolate in a candy bar. To me there isn't a philosophical idea that
isn't to do with food. Toasted marshmallows, late at night, when I first
read Wittgenstein. I can still remember the taste of 'The world is all
that is the case.' It tasted good, it still tastes good, that moment of
understanding something. But *applying* it? Well, that's different, the
world not offering so many opportunities for that sort of thing. Arts and
humanities! Philosophy! What's the point in America, where the only
philosophy you'll ever encounter is the philosophy of making money.
In my case by taking off T-shirts. In fact, not even taking them off – I'm
too up-market for that. I have only to hint there are situations in which
I *would* show my breasts to certain people, certain *rich* people, that they
do indeed exist under there, but for now it's enough to suggest their
shape, hint at their shape, in a T-shirt. Often it will have to be wet. By
soaking my T-shirts in water I make my living. It's true. Little to do
with the life of ideas.

She smiles.

Spoilt. Spoilt doesn't say it, though that's what people say about
Americans, and spoilt, I suppose, is what I was till lunchtime, till I
made this ridiculous offer. A young idiot's suicidal offer with which she
is now going to have to learn to live.

And A Nightingale Sang . . . follows the wartime experiences of a working-class family in Newcastle.

Helen is the slightly crippled older daughter of the family. She meets a married soldier who assures her that his marriage is over and she moves in with him much to the horror of her relations. In this speech Helen is talking directly to the audience.

And A Nightingale Sang . . . *by C. P. Taylor*

Helen *(to audience)*   On the next morning, the Wednesday, it was on
the wireless. They'd landed in Normandy. . . . They were already miles
and miles inside France. . . . But all I could think of was meeting
Norman, that night. . . . He was going to try to come back for the
evening from Durham. . . . We hadn't seen each other for weeks . . .
weeks. . . . When he was away. . . . Sometimes I couldn't stand it. . . . I
was packing his other tunic . . . to take to him. . . . That morning. . . .
He could go right back to Durham. . . . And I saw he'd left some papers
. . . and his pay book . . . in his tunic. . . . Eee . . . I said to myself. . . .
He's a careless bugger. . . . Doesn't even look after his pay book. . . . I
just looked inside . . . I don't know why I looked. . . . And it bloody hit
us. . . . His wife's name was there . . . who he was paying his marriage
allowance to . . . and then . . . an allowance to one child. . . . I kept
going back to the page. . . . To make sure . . . I couldn't believe it
wasn't a mistake. . . . But it was there, right enough. . . . One child . . .
Matthew Peter. . . . I washed up the dishes. . . . And went into Parsons
. . . I just went through the day . . . I was acting full of it. . . . The lasses
in the Blade shop said to us. . . . What had come over us. . . . I was so
cheery. . . . I couldn't bear to go home to me Mam's. . . . Instead . . . I
went to the station . . . to wait for Norman's train. . . . If he was coming.
. . . Waited for hours. . . . Men kept looking at us. . . . Especially the
Yanks. . . . One of them offered us a bar of chocolate . . . I just stared
right through him. . . . In the end . . . I gave up . . . I went to our
bench in Eldon Square. . . . And he was bloody there. . . . Sitting on our
bench . . .

Beryl is one of five characters who are all enjoying a solitary afternoon in the same park. They become involved in an unwitting game of musical chairs – each hoping to avoid enforced contact with one another by changing benches. Beryl has just moved from her bench and starts explaining to the stranger next to her why.

Confusions *by Alan Ayckbourn*

Beryl *(sitting)* Thanks. Sorry, only the man over there won't stop talking. I wanted to read this in peace. I couldn't concentrate. He just kept going on and on about his collections or something. I normally don't mind too much, only if you get a letter like this, you need all your concentration. You can't have people talking in your ear – especially when you're trying to decipher writing like this. He must have been stoned out of his mind when he wrote it. It wouldn't be unusual. Look at it. He wants me to come back. Some hopes. To him. He's sorry, he didn't mean to do what he did, he won't do it again I promise, etc., etc. I seem to have heard that before. It's not the first time, I can tell you. And there's no excuse for it, is there? Violence. I mean, what am I supposed to do? Keep going back to that? Every time he loses his temper he . . . I mean, there's no excuse. A fracture, you know. It was nearly a compound fracture. That's what they told me.

Indicating her head.

Right here. You can practically see it to this day. Two X-rays. I said to him when I got home, I said, 'You bastard, you know what you did to my head?' He just stands there. The way he does. 'Sorry,' he says, 'I'm ever so sorry.' I told him. I said, 'You're a bastard, that's what you are. A right, uncontrolled, violent, bad-tempered bastard.' You know what he said? He says, 'You call me a bastard again and I'll smash your stupid face in.' That's what he says. I mean, you can't have a rational, civilized discussion with a man like that, can you? He's a right bastard. My friend Jenny, she says, 'You're a looney, leave him for God's sake. You're a looney.' Who needs that? You tell me one person who needs that? Only where do you go? I mean, there's all my things – my personal things. All my – everything. He's even got my bloody Post Office book. I'll finish up back there, you wait and see. I must be out of my tiny mind. Eh. Sometimes I just want to jump down a deep hole and forget it. Only I know that bastard'll be waiting at the bottom. Waiting to thump the life out of me. Eh?

A young Irish girl returns from a holiday in Israel pregnant. She claims that it is an immaculate conception. As the press and tourists flock to her town her priest struggles to overcome his doubt and truly have faith. Teresa is young, frail and disarmingly simple. She inspires a protective attitude in most people apart from her own mother. In this scene she is explaining to her local priest what actually happened in the Holy Land.

Tuesday's Child *by Terry Johnson and Kate Lock*

Teresa In the Holy Land. Well, I've told you about the camel. I'm clinging on for dear life while this Arab with no teeth marches me up and down the hill. There's this saddle thing you've to grip between your legs: I was bruised for a week. And at the end of it the camel will not sit down and it's not an easy thing getting off a camel when you've been celebrating ancestors, so Danny and your man, the Arab, have to lift me down between them. Then the Arab tries to kiss me and Danny yells out, then the Arab tries to kiss Danny and Danny yells out even more.

Then Father O'Hagen got back and marched us off down the hill. It was baking hot. What with the wine and the camel ride I was feelin' a bit dizzy so they went on ahead to the Church of the Annunciation. I went in on my own a bit after. Oh Father, it's a beautiful church. It was so cool inside; I put my forehead against a stone pillar to stop the burning and I felt more alive than I've ever felt; you know those moments you have. I went down some stone steps and into the most beautiful corner. It was quiet and hidden and filled with the most wonderful light from a stained-glass window up above. I sat in the little stone alcove and listened to the voices of the others in the church. They sounded centuries away. You see, Father, we'd been rushing about in the heat all day, sweating indecently, laughing at Dan's fooling and drinking the wine and going up and down on camels . . . and suddenly it's cool and quiet and all that rush and tumble is gone. Except that it hasn't, I am full of it. I came over all peculiar. I felt dizzy again. A bit faint. Everything looks red for a bit but when it clears I can see this boy lookin' at me . . . This boy is just a boy but he's the most beautiful boy. He's quite short and has a cheeky sort of a smile: a bit like yours when you're with the little ones, but a far more beautiful face. And he smiles at me. And all the tumble in my mind and all the heat in my body sort of got mixed up together, and that smile seemed to reach down inside me and turn me inside out. It was almost indecent somehow, and sort of painful. But it was a pain so sweet I could have had it go on for ever. But then it was gone and so was the boy. For a while I couldn't move at all; I'd never felt so . . . so . . . You know how it was for St Teresa when the angel pierced her heart with an arrow and left her in ecstasy? . . . Well, it was like that.

Jean is the mother of Verity, an unbalanced child who is not actually retarded – therefore there is no definable place for her within the medical or social services. The family are left to cope with Verity's increasingly difficult behaviour on their own.

Jean has just been denied help by the social services. The social worker assures her that they all feel she is 'managing wonderfully well'.

Find Me *by Olwen Wymark*

Jean What are we going to do? Dear God, what are we going to do? Managing! Perhaps it would be better for all of us if we couldn't manage. Then they'd have to do something. Maybe if I became an alcoholic . . . I could. My God, I think I could sometimes.

Pause.

When I go next door to Suzanne's some nights and we sit and get a bit tight together on whisky and talk about all sorts of things and laugh – just for a little while I can forget. The thoughts stop going round and round in my head. The relief of just feeling like an ordinary person. The relief. Supposing when Miss Everitt Social Services came round today she'd found me dead drunk on the floor. 'Dear me, Mrs Taylor, you're not managing wonderfully well today.'

Pause.

Imagine your own child driving you to drink. Your own child that you love.

Pause.

I don't even know if I do love her. I don't know what I feel. Pity – oh, pity for her. Why did it have to happen? Poor Verity. Poor, poor baby.

Pause.

But fear too. She seems to like to frighten me – enjoys it. She never does it to Edward. I really think sometimes she hates me. And he's so good to her – so patient and kind. All those holidays he takes her on. He doesn't talk much about them afterwards but I know, I know she crucifies him. And I feel mean and cowardly because I didn't go too.

Pause.

And guilty. Did I do it? Was it my fault? When I was pregnant with her – all those weeks when she was inside me I thought she was so safe. Nothing could hurt her and yet all the time. . . . Was it me? Did I – contaminate her? Oh God. . . .

She stops herself.

She was so beautiful when she was a baby. Even now sometimes when you look at her when she's asleep. When I'm out with her sometimes I wish she was ugly. Deformed or crippled. Something people could *see*. Then they would pity her too. Instead of getting nervous and embarrassed and moving away from us as if we were lepers. Oh God, will nobody help us? Can't anybody help us?

Road is an episodic play set in a derelict street in Lancashire where unemployment and despair are rife. Throughout the play different characters reveal the state of their lives.

Clare is the young girlfriend of Joey. He sees no point in living and has retreated to bed where he intends to starve himself to death. Clare joins him, not really understanding the purpose of the protest, but determined to stay with him. The speech is a response to his question: 'Why are you here anyway?'

Road *by Jim Cartwright*

Clare   I don't know. I suppose I don't know what else to do. Every day's the same now. You were my only hobby really, now you're out of it, seems mad to carry on, all me ambition's gone. I filled in a *Honey* quiz last week. 'Have you got driving force?' I got top marks all round. But where can I drive it, Joe? I lost my lovely little job. My office job. I bloody loved going in there you know. Well you do know, I told you about it every night. I felt so sweet and neat in there. Making order out of things. Being skilful. Tackling an awkward situation here and there. The boss smiling at me, telling me I was a good worker. Feeling the lovely light touch of morning when I went out to work. To have a destination. The bus stop, then the office, then the work on the desk, the day's tiny challenge. I mean tiny compared to proper big company work. But I loved it. Exercise to my body, my imagination, my general knowledge. Learning life's little steps. Now I'm saggy from tip to toe. Every day's like swimming in ache. I can't stand wearing the same clothes again and again. Re-hemming, stitching, I'm sick with it, Joe. I'm the bottom of the barrel. I must be. How many letters have I writ? A bloody book's worth, and only ten replies, each the same really. Seven bleeding photo-bleeding-copied. I heard my mum cry again last night. My room's cold. I can't buy my favourite shampoo. Everybody's poor and sickly-white. Oh Joe! Joe! Joe!

The Castle is set during the Crusades. While the men are away fighting, the women form a Utopian society in which there is no place for the men when they return.

Skinner is a radical lesbian feminist who has been having an affair with the Lady of the Manor. Outraged at being rejected in favour of a man, Skinner seeks revenge by murdering a male worker. The speech takes place at her trial. Throughout the speech she is searching for her lover who is in the courtroom.

The Castle *by Howard Barker*

Skinner They have this way you see, of relating the torture to the offence – the things they say – you wouldn't – are you in here, I can't see – put your hand up I can't – am I being reasonable enough for you, not shouting am I, actually I'm half dead – where are you sitting, I –

(She looks around.) I call it daylight but it's relative – I WANT TO SEE YOUR HAND — Can I have a stool or not?

*A **Man** goes to fetch it.*

NOT ONE WITH A SPIKE IN THE MIDDLE! They think of everything – they do – imaginations – you should see the – INVENTION DOWN THERE – makes you gasp the length of their hatred – the uncoiled length of hatred – mustn't complain though – was I complaining – was I – I beg pardon – I have this – tone which – thanks to your expertise is mollified a little.

*The **Man** returns with a stool.*

WHAT DOES THAT DO, BITE YOUR ARSE?

(She looks at it, on the ground.) Looks harmless, looks a harmless little stool, boring bit of carpentry. DON'T BELIEVE IT!

(She goes towards it, extends her fingers gingerly.) Spring trap!

(She leaps back.) Spring trap! Legs fly up and grip your head, seen stools like that before, didn't think I'd fall for that, did you, not really, didn't think I'd –

(She sits on it, in utter exhaustion.) You have to kill them, don't you? Death they understand. Death is their god, not love. Because after he was dead they built nothing, for one day, for one day THEY BUILT NOTHING. And because all things decay, in actual fact for one day the castle went backwards! I mean – by virtue of erosion and the usual rot – there was less castle on Monday than on Sunday. And what did that? DEATH DID! I call it death, they call it murder, they call it battle, I call it slaughter etcetera, etcetera, the word is just a hole down which all things can drop – I mean, I put a stop to him. *(Pause.)* And he was quite a nice man, as far as they – there is a limit to those even of the best intentions – he talked of mutual pleasure – really, the banality! It really hurt my ears – after what we had – to talk of – MUTUAL PLEASURE – can you believe – the very words are . . . *(She dries.)*

Whale Music is a play based on the interaction of women with one another – the pregnant Caroline providing the central point around which they pivot.

Stella is a warm, exuberant but cynical woman who rarely lowers her defensive barriers. In this speech she explains to Caroline the reason for her behaviour at the dance the night before.

Whale Music *by Anthony Minghella*

Stella   They do exist, Caroline. It's not my imagination. There's something I do, have done before. If I land a really three-star macho man . . . you know, the whole image . . . never stops telling you what a great time he's going to give you. He's going to make you really cry out, you know, like drowning . . . and all this whispered or licked at you across his MG or yelled in your face on his Yamaha, a great gob full of, whatever, garlic, or grease or fag smoke, and fucking Brut – always Brut or Prick or Stud or Come or whatever they can dream up to call that very unpleasant smell that hides that other very unpleasant smell which is the smell of them getting turned on to you – and they want to get it up through your tights in some car park so that they don't have to cope with you afterwards, you know, because they have no feeling, nothing . . . dead eyes, dead bodies. So what I do is this. I give him . . . Mr Godsgift . . . I give him the real Penthouse cliché, right. Lick my lips, touch myself, scream a bit, play scared when he steps out of his knickers, I mean – awestruck – and I get so very excited in the first number. I always try and break things in his bedroom – preferably something expensive – because I'm so wild for it – and I give out all the words. And I can get it done in a few minutes and, well, there he is, slack-jawed, grinning, notching me up on the barrel, three-quarters asleep. So I leave him for a few minutes, then kiss him like it was love – and then I get going on him for round two. Well! Bit of a laugh, bit nervous now, Mr Godsgift, bit sheepish . . . but I'm good, OK, and he gets some response and it's going to be a great story for his pals in the morning: 'You should have seen this slag – she couldn't get enough of it!' And he makes ride number two, sometimes makes ride number three, perhaps, but he's losing and he's worried and he's sore and he's fucking terrified, and the NEXT time I make certain he falls apart. I'm surprised. I'm very disappointed he can't make it. I even get angry with him. And then I get dressed and come home and stand under the shower and scrub him off me and if I could stand boiling water I'd boil myself clean to the marrow.

Sandra is one of a group of women, living in Nottingham, whose husband is still away fighting in the Pacific War. The play is set in the 100 days between V.E. and V.J. days.

Sandra informs her family that she is pregnant, but refuses to reveal the name of the father. This leads to a huge family row. The speech takes place after they have all left the house, leaving Sandra alone.

Touched *by Stephen Lowe*

Sandra I took a picnic. What I could scrape together. Bread. My
ration of cheese. Flask of tea. I took it all nice. Lace tablecloth. I stood,
looking through the barbed wire. I walked off when they came out.
Bent shouldered men in a crisp March. March. March. I marched off
at a good pace. He was right behind me. Perhaps he spoke. I don't
know. I had to find a certain place, that I must have found before, but I
was still surprised when we came upon it. I must have found it earlier,
but I couldn't believe it was there, that I had looked for it, that I was
returning to this place. I thought the ground is hard and dry. It won't
stain my tablecloth, won't stain my dress. This is fine, anything can
happen here, in the lace of these trees, and it won't stain. I knelt, and
began to unpack my bag. I knew I could walk away and it may never
have happened. I laid out the lace cloth, wiped out the creases, set out
the flask, the food, around the edges like for a child's party. I stood and
walked carefully around the outside of the edge. I looked up. I faced
him. We stood apart. It suddenly was a very hot day. I felt faint. I
thought, I'll fall. Look at him, I thought, look at him. He began to
speak. His voice rose. Anger? Hate? I couldn't understand what he was
saying. The crispness was going. The fog was settling in. His voice grew
louder. He was undoing his clothing. His trousers. I knew what he was
saying. He was giving me orders. He was . . . giving me . . . orders. I
looked at him, and I knew the lace was there, the food was there. I
looked at him. I waited. Slowly his voice faded away. He stood there,
unbuttoned, sad, clumsy against the lace, like a puppet with the strings
broken. I spoke. I think they were the first words I spoke, and the last
bar one. You – I pointed to him – PRISONER. He looked away.
Frowned. Frowned like a little child. He understood me. It hurt me.
NO, I said. I shook my head, meaning no. He looked up. I crossed the
white to him. I put out my hands to him. I reached into his crumpled
clothes, I touched him. Touched. I felt the shiver. The pulse. He is real.
I . . . he . . . we are both here. The roughness of his clothes, the softness
of the man's skin. I want to go down in front of him. I want him to go
down in front of me. I want things I've never dreamed of, sins I have
always feared. I pray. A second's prayer. Not to ask, Lord, but to
thank. I want to be free, and I am free. I am real. I am alive. The Lord
is my shepherd. I shall not want. He maketh me to lie down in green
pastures: he leadeth me beside the still waters. Thou preparest a table
before me in the presence of thine enemies; my cup runneth over. Lord.
Holy mother. Holy child. The Rainbow. The Rainbow.

In Nottingham in 1944 a cinema owner and his young usherette act out during the course of their day their fantasies of Vivien Leigh and Robert Taylor. In counterpoint a relationship is developing between Jane, an older woman, and a young U.S. soldier. Both women have just been given a pair of nylons by the men.

Stars *by Stephen Lowe*

Jane puts on her stockings.

Girl *(ecstatic)*   Oh! You can't guess what this means to me, after all these years of dreary, dreary stockings. And everybody's saying you're lucky to have a pair of them for best. And now – lovely things to wear. That's what's so awful about this war. A pretty girl forced to wear flannelettes, and utility suits. No make-up. No nylons. No nothing. It isn't fair. You've got nothing to look back on. You can't say to yourself, well I did look nice then. Even if you get the top half decent, underneath you're wearing summat'd make a Bevin-lad blush. If you got knocked down, or hit by a bomb, honest, you'd be ashamed. But being put in an ambulance wi' nylons on, well then they know they're dealing with somebody wi' a bit of class. Class. When I went straight out o' school into lace market, in '40, I remember me mam bringing home little snippets of Nottingham lace, black, white, blue, all colours, too small for you to do ought wi' but hoard them like precious jewels, but I thought, I'll soon be old enough to buy some underskirts laced round with this. There, aren't they lovely?

The play is a two-hander based on the letters between Sylvia Plath, the poet, and her mother. It covers the years from her first days at college, through her marriage to Ted Hughes and to her eventual suicide.

The speech is a diary entry of Sylvia's which her mother found when collating the book *Letters Home* (Faber) on which this play is based.

Letters Home *by Rose Leiman Goldenberg* from *Sylvia Plath*

Aurelia *(a decision. To herself, to **Sylvia,** to the audience; gathering resolution, strength).*

November 13, 1949.

As of today I have decided to keep a diary again – just a place where I can write my thoughts and opinions when I have a moment. Somehow I have to keep and hold the rapture of being *seventeen*. Every day is so precious. I feel infinitely sad at the thought of all this time melting farther and farther away from me as I grow older. *Now, now* is the perfect time of my life.

I still do not know myself. Perhaps I never will. But I feel free – unbound by responsibility, I still can come up to my own private room, with my drawings hanging on the walls, and pictures pinned up over my bureau – a room suited to me, uncluttered and peaceful. I love the quiet lines of the furniture, the two bookcases filled with poetry books and fairy tales saved from childhood. (. . .)

I am afraid of getting older. I am afraid of getting married. Spare me from cooking three meals a day – spare me from the relentless cage of routine and rote. I want to be *free* – free to know people and their backgrounds – free to move to different parts of the world. I want, I think, to be omniscient. I think I would like to call myself 'the girl who wanted to be God' . . . perhaps I am *destined* to be classified and qualified. But, oh, I cry out against it. I am I.

I love my flesh, my face, my limbs. I have erected in my mind an image of myself, idealistic and beautiful. Is not that image, free from blemish, the true self – the true perfection? (. . .)

There will come a time when I must face myself at last. Even now I dread the big choices

which loom up in my life. I am afraid. I feel uncertain. I am not as wise as I have thought.

I can now see, as from a valley, the roads lying open for me but I cannot see the end – the consequences.

Oh, I love *now*, with all my fears and forebodings, for now I still am not completely molded. *I am strong*.

My life is still just beginning!

Shirley is a middle-aged Liverpudlian housewife. As she prepares her husband's dinner she reminisces over her early years of bringing up her children, who now seem to have little time or understanding for her.

Shirley Valentine *by Willy Russell*

Shirley An' then our Brian is supposed to say somethin' like: 'Well we must go an' find a lowly cattle shed an' stay in there.' Then he's supposed to go off pullin' the donkey, an' the Virgin Mary behind him. But he didn't. Well, I don't know if it's the Virgin Mary, gettin' up our Brian's nose, because she's spent the whole scene wavin' to her Mother or whether it was just that our Brian suddenly realized that the part of Joseph wasn't as big as it had been cracked up to be. But whatever it was, instead of goin' off pullin' the donkey, he suddenly turned to the little Innkeeper an' yelled at him – 'Full up? Full up? But we booked!' Well the poor little Innkeeper didn't know what day of the week it was. He's lookin' all round the hall for someone to rescue him an' his bottom lip's beginnin' to tremble an' our Brian's goin' – 'Full up? I've got the wife outside, waitin' with the donkey. She's expectin' a baby any minute now, there's snow everywhere in six foot drifts an' you're tryin' to tell me that you're full up?' Well the top brass on the front row are beginnin' to look a bit uncomfortable – they're beginnin' to turn an' look at the headmaster an' our Brian's givin' a perfect imitation of his father, on a bad day; he's beratin' anythin' that dares move. The little Innkeeper's lip is goin' ten to the dozen an' the Virgin Mary's in floods of tears on the donkey. Well the Innkeeper finally grasps that the script is well out of the window an' that he has to do somethin' about our Brian. So he steps forward an' he says, 'Listen Mate, listen! I was only jokin'. We have got room really. Y' can come in if y' want.' An' with that the three of them disappeared into the Inn. End of Nativity play an' the end of our Brian's actin' career.

Fen follows the lives of the women who work the potato harvest in the Fenlands. Margaret is a middle-aged woman, attending a Baptist meeting. Although this is the only time her character appears in the play, it is important to read the whole piece to understand the structure of the Fenland society.

She has been called upon to share the experiences which have led to her conversion to Christ.

Fen *by Caryl Churchill*

Margaret   I thought I would be nervous but I'm not. Because Jesus is giving me strength to speak. I don't know where to begin because I've been unhappy as long as I can remember. My mother and father were unhappy too. I think my grandparents were unhappy. My father was a violent man. You'd hear my mother, you'd say, 'Are you all right, mum?' But that's a long time ago. I wasn't very lucky in my marriage. So after that I was on my own except I had my little girl. Some of you knew her. But for those of you who didn't, she couldn't see. I thought at first that was why she couldn't learn things but it turned out to be in her head as well. But I taught her to walk, they said she wouldn't but she did. She slept in my bed, she wouldn't let me turn away from her, she'd put her hand on my face. It was after she died I started drinking, which has been my greatest sin and brought misery to myself and to those who love me. I betrayed them again and again by saying I would give it up, but the drink would have me hiding a little away. But my loving sisters in Christ stood beside me. I thought if God wants me he'll give me a sign, because I couldn't believe he really would want someone as terrible as me. I thought if I hear two words today, one beginning with M for Margaret, my name, and one with J for Jesus, close together, then I'll know how close I am to him. And that very afternoon I was at Mavis's house and her little boy was having his tea, and he said, 'More jam, mum.' So that was how close Jesus was to me, right inside my heart. That was when I decided to be baptised. But I slid back and had a drink again and the next day I was in despair. I thought God can't want me, nobody can want me. And a thrush got into my kitchen. I thought if that bird can fly out, I can fly out of my pain. I stood there and I watched, I didn't open another window, there was just the one window open. The poor bird beat and beat around the room, the tears were running down my face. And at last it found the window and went straight out into the air. I cried tears of joy because I knew Jesus would save me. So I went to Malcolm and said baptise me now because I'm ready. I want to give myself over completely to God so there's nothing else of me left, and then the pain will be gone and I'll be saved. Without the love of my sisters I would never have got through.

Ourselves Alone is set during the present 'troubles' in Ulster and shows how three women are affected and manipulated by the violent politics of their families, husbands and lovers.

Josie, in her late twenties, acts as a courier passing messages between various factions of the IRA. Having been desperately in love with a married terrorist for years, she begins an affair with an Englishman who wishes to join the IRA. In this speech she describes to him the beginning of her affair with Cathal.

Ourselves Alone *by Anne Devlin*

Josie *(speaking aloud)*   Bus stop posts; manhole covers; telephone kiosk doors; traffic signs; corrugated iron fencing; and old doors, wood is best not glass; especially if you don't have an upturned bus or lorry. And a tape measure is useful too, to measure the mouth of the street. . . . He held one end of the tape and I had the other. It was the first time I'd ever seen him. He kept shouting at me to hold still. Hurry up. Move quickly. Find the rope, nails, wood. He was so precise. And I kept coming back with what he wanted every time. . . . All day we ran about measuring, hammering, securing, until towards evening we needed only two slim posts and it was finished. I remember we rushed off to the park to uproot some young trees, saplings the Corporation planted. We were high up on the bank when a woman passed. She was pushing a pram; a pregnant woman in a headscarf, then she waved. It was my first whole day with him. 'It's my wife,' he said. Safe. I'm safe from him. The sight of her large and alone, thoughts on her child in the womb and in the pram were battleship enough to keep me away. Until minutes later I slipped, slid down the wet bank after him and came to a halt. 'I can't get down,' I said. And he reached out his hand . . . I wasn't safe. I was lost.

Joe returns, dressed. He watches from the doorway.

Making Noise Quietly is one of a trilogy of short plays showing the profound effect a chance meeting has on the protagonists involved. They are thematically linked by the twentieth-century wars.

Helene has befriended a British soldier and his disturbed stepson on holiday. A survivor of the Nazi death camps, she refuses to allow the soldier to denigrate himself for beating his son and tells him of her experience of true cruelty.

Making Noise Quietly *by Robert Holman*

Helene buttons her sleeve.

Helene   He was a soldier. A guard. He was at the station when we arrived. He even helped my mother by not pushing her. I was ten years old.

A slight pause.

He walked beside me through the gates. Then there must have been a mistake because, at the hut we were taken to, we children and women had to get undressed in front of him. He was so embarrassed. I was too. My mother told me not to be silly. Then a female guard arrived and the mistake was put right. But a minute later a message came. I was to get dressed. I had to put on another girl's clothes because, by now, mine were at the bottom of the heap. I so wanted to be clean that I cried. My mother pushed me to the door. She pushed me away. I saw him outside. I have tried to forget his kindness, but somehow it is impossible.

A slight pause.

The next day he came and asked me what I liked to do. I told him painting. I made that up because it was really my brother who was the painter, but at that moment I could not think. He brought me paper from his quarters and some crayons. I had to draw him. He smiled and pulled faces—I had to draw these too. I was hiding my paper from him because of this lie. But I liked him very much. He told me his name was Kurt. He was twenty-four.

A slight pause.

One day he took me to his billet. My sketches were up on the wall by his bunk. It was then he told me I had been lying to him. But I sat down on the stool as usual. And, with a little cane, he flicked at my legs as I drew. He looked so, so angry. I saw my friend Kurt for the first time. I think he wanted me to cry but I could not because, by now, my body was so dried up. We did not have tears. He told me I would pay for what I had done. He had my head shaved again. I had to draw him, on my scalp, with a razor blade.

A slight pause.

When I was better he had my head shaved again. You see what you nearly do to me?